UNDERSTANDING
THE HEARTBEAT OF JESUS

UNDERSTANDING
THE HEARTBEAT OF JESUS

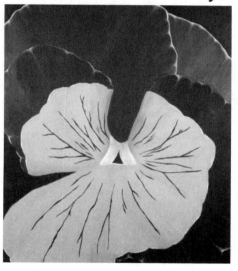

Jill Briscoe
. . .

For Her. For God. For Real.
faithfulwoman.com

Faithful Woman is an imprint of
Cook Communications Ministries, Colorado Springs, Colorado 80918
Cook Communications, Paris, Ontario
Kingsway Communications, Eastbourne, England

UNDERSTANDING THE HEARTBEAT OF JESUS
© 2001 by Briscoe Ministries, Inc.

First Printing, 1993
Printed in the United States of America

1 2 3 4 5 6 7 8 9 10 Printing/Year 05 04 03 02 01

Sr. Editor: Craig Bubeck
Cover Painting: Sara Blackford

Library of Congress Cataloging-in-Publication Data

Briscoe, Jill P.
Understanding the Heartbeat of Jesus/Jill Briscoe

    p. cm.
ISBN 0-78143-658-3

Recommended Dewy Decimal Classification: 248.843
Suggested Subject Heading: PERSONAL CHRISTIANITY FOR WOMEN

Contents

Special recognition and thanks to Beth Donigan Seversen for assistance in researching and formulating parts of this study guide, and to Rhea Briscoe for her reformatting and typing work.

Before You Begin

People who gather together for Bible study are likely to be at different places in their spiritual lives, and their study materials should be flexible enough to meet their varying needs. This book is designed to do just that! It may be used as a Bible study guide for groups, whether they be held in homes or churches, or it may be used by individuals for personal Bible study. Each lesson is designed with five study process sections, allowing for a great deal of flexibility according to your study needs.

These studies will help you learn not only valuable new truths from the Bible, but also the process of digging out such truths for yourself. Furthermore, beyond learning what the Bible says, you will learn how to use Scripture to deepen your relationship with Jesus Christ by applying it and obeying it. In addition, developing leaders will learn how to disciple in a nonthreatening setting.

What You'll Need

For each study you will need a Bible and this study guide. You might also want to have a notebook in which to record your thoughts and discoveries from your personal study and group meetings. A notebook could also be used to record prayer requests from the group.

Options for Group Use

Different groups are made up of people at various stages of spiritual growth. Here are a few suggestions to get you started, but be aware of how God might use your own creativity and sensitivity to the group's particular needs:

1. Spend 5-15 minutes at the beginning of the group time introducing yourselves and having group members answer

an icebreaker question. (Sample icebreaker questions are included under Tips for Leaders.)

2. Extend the prayer time to include sharing of prayer requests, praise items, or things group members have learned recently in their times of personal Bible study.

TIPS FOR LEADERS

Preparation

1. Pray for the Holy Spirit's guidance as you study, that you will be equipped to teach the lesson and make it appealing and applicable.

2. Read through the entire lesson and any Bible passages or verses that are mentioned. Answer all of the lesson's questions.

3. Become familiar enough with the lesson that, if time in the group is running out, you know which questions could most easily be left out.

4. Gather all the items you will need for the study: name tags, extra pens, extra Bibles.

The Meeting

1. Start and end on time.

2. Have everyone wear a name tag until group members know one another's names.

3. Have all members introduce themselves or ask regular attendees to introduce guests.

4. For each meeting, pick an icebreaker question or another activity to help group members get to know one another better.

5. Use any good ideas to make everyone feel comfortable.

The Discussion

1. Ask the questions, but try to let the group answer. Don't be afraid of silence. Reword the question if it is unclear to the group. Only as a last resort should you answer it yourself to clarify.

2. Encourage everyone to participate. If someone is shy, purposely ask that person to answer a nonthreatening question or give an opinion. If someone tends to monopolize the discussion, thank that person for contributing and ask if someone else has anything to add. (Or ask that person to make the coffee!)

3. If someone gives an incorrect answer, don't bluntly or tactlessly tell him or her so. If it is partly right, reinforce that. Ask if anyone else has any thoughts on the subject. (Disagree agreeably.)

4. Avoid tangents. If someone is getting off the subject, ask that person to connect the point to the lesson.

5. Don't feel threatened if someone asks a question you can't answer. Tell the person you don't know but will find out before the next meeting—then be sure to find out! Or ask if someone would like to research and present the answer at the group's next meeting.

Icebreaker Questions

The purpose of these icebreaker questions is to help the people in your group get to know one another over the course of the study. The questions you use when your group members don't know one another very well should be very general and nonthreatening. As time goes on, your questions can become more focused and specific. Always give group members the option of passing if they think a question is too personal.

What do you like to do for fun?

What is your favorite season? dessert? book?

What would be your ideal vacation?

What exciting thing happened to you this week?

What was the most memorable thing you did with your family when you were a child?

What one word best describes the way you feel today?

Tell three things you are thankful for.

Imagine that your house is on fire. What three things would you try to take with you on your way out?

If you were granted one wish, what would it be?

What experience of your past would you most enjoy reliving?

What quality do you most appreciate in a friend?

What is your pet peeve?

What is something you are learning to do or trying to get better at?

What is your greatest hope?

What is your greatest fear?

What one thing would you like to change about yourself?

What has been the greatest accomplishment of your life?

What has been the greatest disappointment of your life?

Need More Help?

Here is a list of books that contain helpful information on leading discussions and working in groups:

How to Lead Small Group Bible Studies (NavPress, 1982).
Creative Bible Learning for Adults, Monroe Marlowe and Bobbie Reed (Regal, 1977).
Getting Together, Em Griffin (InterVarsity Press, 1982).
Good Things Come in Small Groups (InterVarsity Press, 1985).

ONE LAST THOUGHT

This study book is a tool you can use whether you have one or one hundred people who want to study the Bible, and for that matter, whether or not you have a teacher. Indeed, don't wait for a brilliant Bible study leader to appear—most such teachers acquired their skills by starting with a book like this and learning as they went along. Torrey said, "The best way to begin, is to begin." Happy beginnings!

CHAPTER ONE

Jesus' Early Years

. . .

Leader ▪ welcomes group and makes sure everyone knows each other's name. It's good if everyone has their own Bible to read. The leader may want to bring a few along.

Leader ▪ opens in prayer and designates three readers.

FOOD FOR THOUGHT

Leader ▪ reads text.

Let's try and "hear" the heartbeat of Jesus. What motivated Him? What moved Him to come to earth from heaven, fully cognizant of exactly the sort of treatment He would receive at the hands of people like us: human beings He Himself had created. Let's look at the record of His early years spent on our little globe.

What Christmas story do you enjoy most and why? (Choose and read one, then share.)

Gabriel and Mary (Luke 1:26-38)

Mary and Elizabeth (Luke 1:39-56)

The Shepherds (Luke 2:8-20)

The Wise Men (Matthew 2:1-12)

Joseph and the Angel (Matthew 1:18-25)

Reader 1 ▪ I cannot help but wonder what Jesus looked like as He slept, what games He played with His little friends, what scrapes He suffered on His little knees that His mother bathed with tender care! Yet Scripture closes the curtains firmly on us, allowing only His earthly family to witness the little boy's growth from babyhood. We do know, however, that "Jesus grew in wisdom and stature, and in favor with God and men" (Luke 2:52).

What do you think "Jesus grew in wisdom and stature, and in favor with God and men" means?

Leader ▪ leads

DIGGING DEEPER

1. Let's look more closely at the recorded stories of Jesus' infancy and birth. Read the following incidents in Luke 2:21-52 as an overview, and list all the information Luke gives his readers about Jesus' identity.

   Luke 2:21

   Luke 2:22-35

   Luke 2:36-40

   Luke 2:41-52

   Read Luke 2:21-40.

   Notice the names and descriptions applied to Jesus.

2. Why was it necessary for Jesus to meet the requirements of the law? (cf. 2:21, 39; Gal. 4:4ff)

3.   What did the Holy Spirit confirm to Simeon? (cf. Luke 2:25ff; Isa. 42:1)

4.   Whose salvation would be affected by Jesus, the Lord's Christ? (cf. Luke 2:30-32)

5.   What effect did Simeon foretell Jesus would have on men? (cf. Luke 2:32-38)

6.   From studying the context, what do you think "the falling and rising of many in Israel" means? (cf. Luke 2:34) Check your answer against a commentary.

7.   How will Jesus the Messiah be received? (cf. Luke 2:34-35)

8.   What will His suffering reveal? Is it possible to be neutral about who Jesus is?

9.   What do you notice about the two people privileged to first recognize Jesus as the long awaited Messiah?

Reader 2 ■ When Jesus was twelve, He and His family went to Jerusalem at Passover to celebrate His religious coming of age. His parents were fulfilling the requirements of the Law and bringing their son to confirmation. From now on their boy would be held fully responsible for His own actions. He was to become a free moral agent. Now Jesus would receive the Law directly and not through His mother and father.

Up to this point, the child would have been taught at Mary's knee, learning to chant psalms, and beginning to hear about Hebrew law and history. It's strange to think of Jesus listening to the stories of Noah and his ark full of animals, Joseph being dumped in a pit by his brothers, and David and Goliath.

Reader 3 ■ When Jesus was around six, He would have started school. I can imagine how eager He would have been to go to the "house of the Book" and learn from the rulers and teachers about the Old Testament. This would be His only textbook! For five years, along with His friends from the village, He would have memorized the Pentateuch, that is, the first five books of Moses. It was said that a Jew knew the Law better than his own name!

And now at the age of twelve He was to be presented to the learned doctors in the temple at Jerusalem and tested by questions arising from His training (Luke 2:41-51). Needless to say, He passed with flying colors! It's funny, isn't it, thinking of Jesus taking exams like our children do?

Perhaps you are a grandparent like I am. Taking your two grandchildren to the supermarket can make you break out in a rash these days! As the kids chase each other around the aisles and disappear for a frightening minute or two, I think of what it must have been like for Joseph and Mary returning from the celebration, to have realized with horror that Jesus was missing. What a relief to find Him safe—but what a typical angry reaction, too.

> "Son, why have You treated us like this? Your father and I have been anxiously searching for You," they exclaimed (Luke 2:48b). Jesus courteously answered His parents' question with another question, "Why were you searching for me? . . . Didn't you know I had to be in my Father's house?" (Luke 2:49)

Leader ▪ leads

DIGGING DEEPER
Read Luke 2:41-52.

1. Where did Mary and Joseph eventually find Jesus and what activity was He engaged in?

2. What can be surmised from this story regarding Jesus' interests, values, and spiritual appetite at age twelve?

3. Reread Mary's comments. What did she and Joseph assume by Jesus' behavior?

4. What does Jesus' reply to his parents imply about His conduct, attitude, and motives?

5. Compare verses 41-42 with verse 51. Why do you think Luke carefully chose these exact words to record this event? (cf. Deut. 5:16; Luke 2:39)

6. In Luke 2:49 we read the first known words of Jesus, the Lord's Christ, the Messiah. How much of His own

identity is He aware of, and how might He have come to this realization?

Leader ▪ What is this all about? Is this a naughty boy who wouldn't come when He was called? A child careless of His parent's feelings? Or is this the God-man coming of age and telling His world in the person of Mary and Joseph that first and foremost He "must" be about His Heavenly Father's business? That though His parents were dearly loved, there was a relationship that superseded even the most important earthly tie. "This is what I 'must' be about," He said. "This" was the heartbeat of Jesus.

If only we could be so firm about our life's direction! To say and mean it—that our relationship with God and the business He would have us to conduct on His behalf comes first, before all earthly responsibilities and that our Father's things supersede our own personal needs and interests. Jesus put "GOD THINGS" first! The things to do with God and His plans and purposes. In other words, the things of His Father were to Him the chief things. How convicting this is to me. So often the things that clutter up my life divert my attention from the eternal things that really matter.

We need to note this heavenly calling, this holy mission, this divine work was to be played out first in Nazareth. After this event was over Jesus went back to Nazareth and subjected himself to Mary and Joseph's authority for another eighteen years! It was here the preparation for His life's work would take place.

Reader 2 ▪ What a mystery it all is! How did Jesus know His identity, and what did He know then? That Jesus had a divine nature is a tenant of our Christian faith. Only a divine being could effect the redemption of the race. So when I think of Jesus going to school I ask myself, why would someone divine have to go to school? If Jesus was God why did He need to be instructed?

To be perfect God yet perfect man does not in any sense mean that Jesus was born a "super-baby"! He was a human baby with a human nature, yet perfect God with God's nature. The mystery of Jesus' divine and human nature is impossible in the end for finite minds to grasp and must be accepted by faith.

Reader 3 ▪ As Jesus grew up He was probably told by His parents of the account of His extraordinary birth. He must have understood that His circumcision was a sign of His particularly unique relationship with God. For all other Jews it had been an outward symbol, understood as a covenant in the context of separation from God by sin. But Jesus knew He came to do all that was necessary to restore man's broken relationship with the Father. Again, Jesus knew He "must" be about His Father's business. For Jesus there was no other way. This was a big MUST. It was not a "maybe," a "should be," or a "hope to be" but a "must be"! It was the whole focus of His whole life.

Leader ▪ In Nazareth Jesus "increased" His grasp of this part of The Plan for His life. He increased in His understanding of just what His Father purposed and what The Plan entailed. At an early age His awareness of this knowledge began and increased until "one moment"—we know not when "He knew" perfectly His origin, identity, and destiny.

As Jesus Christ came to realize His identity so must we. Have we had our "big moment" when we realized and recognized who He REALLY is? Jesus was not merely a good man who came to an untimely end or a deluded person with grandiose ideas about Himself. Jesus was very God of very God, yet very man of very man. Now, maybe even if you don't understand it all, you would be able to accept the facts by faith.

The Bible is a reliable record of these facts, and God intends us to trust the information we read there. Jesus Christ was a historical figure—yet He was also perfect man and God. When I believe that, it will be a big moment for me. I will want to thank Him for coming to procure my reconciliation with a God I have offended by my sin. Then I, like my Savior, will want to say, "I MUST be about my Father's business"—telling my world about the big mystery of His terrible death but glorious resurrection on their behalf!

Leader ■ leads

PRAYING IT THROUGH (25 *MINUTES*)

1. Meditate on Jesus' childhood. Then praise Him for sharing this part of our experience with us and for us.

    Praise God for—

    - the Incarnation

    - Mary's servant spirit

    - Joseph's obedient heart

    - Zechariah and Elizabeth

    - the shepherds and the wise men who all believed the Good News the angel brought.

    Praise Him for His deity and His humanity.
    (5 minutes)

2. Pray for people who—

    - are in cults and who don't accept Jesus' divinity.

> ■ believe Jesus was only a good man.
>
> Pray for missionaries, teachers, radio, and TV; for cassette and tape ministries that are seeking to tell people this Good News. Pray for their financial needs to be met. (*5 minutes*)
>
> 3. Pray for yourself in order that you "must" be about your Father's business. (*5 minutes*)
>
> 4. MEDITATE (*10 minutes*)
>
>   ■ Can you say, "I MUST be about my Father's business"?
>
>   ■ What do you think this means practically for you?

Leader ■ suggests

FOR FURTHER STUDY

1. How did Jesus' obedience to His parents and to God's will as a young boy prepare Him for His future ministry? (cf Luke 22:42; Phil. 2:8; Heb. 5:8-9)

2. Do a concordance study of Jesus' references to God as His Father. What do you learn about Jesus' understanding of His divine relationship to God and His own divinity?

Leader ■ explains

■ ■ ■

TOOL CHEST (*A SUGGESTED OPTIONAL RESOURCE*)

Know Why You Believe by Paul Little, expansion by Marie Little. InterVarsity Press, 1988.

In this updated edition of *Know Why You Believe*, twelve most-asked questions non-Christians grapple with are answered, and the answers backed by compelling evidence. If your acquaintances are struggling with a scientific problem that seems to be preventing them from placing their faith in Christ, the right answer may bring them peace and pave the way for their commitment to Christ. The following chapter titles alone

9

will adequately introduce you to this book's contents:

1. Is Christianity Rational?
2. Is There a God?
3. Is Christ God?
4. Did Christ Rise from the Dead?
5. Is the Bible God's Word?
6. Are the Bible Documents Reliable?
7. Does Archaeology Verify Scripture?
8. Are Miracles Possible?
9. Do Science and Scripture Agree?
10. Why Does God Allow Suffering and Evil?
11. Does Christianity Differ from Other World Religions?
12. Is Christian Experience Valid?

The late Paul Little tried and tested these answers during the 25 years he wrestled intellectually with unbelieving students on college campuses across the United States. Simple yet profound answers to genuine questions that need our response are available in *Know Why You Believe*.

CHAPTER TWO

Jesus and John the Baptist

■ ■ ■

Leader ▪ welcomes group, uses icebreaker, and opens in prayer.

Leader ▪ designates three readers. Can be the same or different from last time.

Leader ▪ begins

FOOD FOR THOUGHT

What is it that brings pleasure to God? What makes Him happy? What makes His heart smile? Jesus!

God had been silent for the previous 400 years of Israel's history. To be without a prophet for such a long time had created a great hunger and longing within many hearts in Israel. And now God had sent John to call people to repentance and to promise that someone greater than himself would come. His ministry drew huge crowds. And always, John pointed them to the Messiah that was coming soon—the One who had chosen to live His life inside our humanity, whose shoes he wasn't fit to carry. "I am not the Christ but am sent ahead of Him," (John 3:28) he said emphatically.

Reader 1. He preached fiercely, and his message stung. He was not afraid to tell everyone in earshot to clean up their acts. He took on the hard-bitten soldiers, the rogues and rascals among the population, and even the leaders of the Jews traveled down from Jerusalem to check him out. All were subjected to the same treatment. He called the Pharisees and Sadducees "a bunch of snakes" and challenged their hypocrisies. He ordered the soldiers and tax collectors to quit ripping people off and be content with their pay. The common people too were called to put their relationships right with each other and confess their sins. The people swarmed to his baptisms convinced the King was well on His way. Then one day the King arrived!

Reader 2. John watched Jesus wade into the water. He was shocked. Jesus was coming to be baptized! "I need to be baptized by You!" he exclaimed. Jesus calmly told John to baptize Him anyway. His baptism was an affirmation of His determination to do the work His Heavenly Father had assigned Him to do. John was well aware Jesus had no sin to confess, but he did what Jesus asked him to do and experienced God's affirmation to his own heart. This man was definitely the One he had been preaching about to the crowds.

Reader 3. The Voice spoke, and John heard it clearly: "This is My beloved Son in whom I am well pleased." At this point the Holy Spirit either appeared in the form of a dove, or as the Apostle John writing his Gospel described it in simile, "the Spirit like a dove" rested on Jesus. John had been told about the Spirit's appearance and that this was the way he was to recognize the Lord's Christ. Now he had

> absolutely no doubts at all that Jesus was "the Lamb
> of God" [who had come to take away the sin of the
> world] (John 1:35).

Leader ▪ leads

TALKING IT OVER (15 MINUTES)

1. Read the story of the doubts John the Baptist had in prison
    concerning Jesus as Messiah (Matthew 11:2-6).

    ▪ Why do you think John was doubting that Jesus was
    the Messiah?

    ▪ What did Jesus say to reassure him? Why do you think
    this was significant?

    ▪ What do we learn from all this?

    Jesus' baptism came at a pivotal point in salvation history.
    The Son of God determined to take on His servant role.
    This role entailed His identifying with the people and
    choosing to obey like a servant. Jesus knew He was the
    loved Son and Servant the Father had promised to sustain,
    and that the Father would help Him face the suffering that
    was ahead as He died for the sins of us all. At His baptism
    Jesus also knew that the Father was publicly presenting
    Him as the expected Messiah.

Leader ▪ leads

DIGGING DEEPER

1. What did John's baptism demonstrate, and how did it
    prepare the people for the coming of the Christ?

2. John quotes Isaiah 40:3 and illustrates personal preparation for the coming of the Lord by picturing the making and remaking or reconstruction of a highway. What proportions should one's preparations take for the Lord's arrival? What do these preparations include?

3. In your own words, what do you think John is asking the people to do?

4. Baptism was a rite the Jews applied to Gentile converts. Where and to whom was John preaching? What offense might have been taken at his preaching?

5. According to John, who was the Lord coming to save? What was the Lord coming to save them from? What further offense might have been taken from John's message?

6. What warning does John issue in Luke 3:7ff? Is it too late for the crowds to receive God's salvation? Why or why not?

7. What false security was John's audience trusting in to save them from "the coming wrath"?

8. Give the sign and result of genuine repentance.

9. Contrast those who accepted and rejected John's message and warning (cf. Luke 3:10-15 and 7:29-30). Compare their responses (cf. Luke 3:10-15 and 7:31-35).

10. John teaches the tax collectors and soldiers two principles to live by which will help them prepare their hearts for the Lord. What are they?

11. How does John help the people differentiate between himself and the Messiah?

12. How does Luke 3:17 explain Jesus' baptism of fire? What are the positive and negative results of Christ's coming?

13. Why is this picture of certain judgment included in the description of the good news John preached?

14. Reread chapter 3:21-23. What two fold confirmation is Jesus given after His baptism, and why is this important in light of what is about to commence in chapters 4 and following? How does Luke 1–3 serve as an introduction for the rest of Luke's Gospel?

15. What would the words from heaven have recalled to a Jewish audience? (cf. Ps. 2:7; Isa. 42:1)

PERSONAL APPLICATION

1. How might John have required you to prepare for the Lord? Are you sharing with those who have nothing? Do you act justly at work?

2. What false security are you trusting in for your salvation? Do you rely on your Christian heritage or good works to be accepted by God?

3. Does John's message offend you? Are you willing to repent and ask Christ to forgive you for your sins and cleanse you of all your unrighteousness? (cf. 1 John 1:9)

SYNOPSIS

In one or two sentences, summarize Luke 3:1-23, John's message and passion. Do you share his heartbeat?

Reader 1 ▪ The next time God audibly voiced His delight in His most loved Son was three years later. As He had affirmed the thirty years in Nazareth at Jesus' baptism, now He affirmed His three years of ministry. Jesus had taken Peter, James, and John up a mountain. When they were quite alone, the Bible says Jesus was transfigured in front of them. It was as if He took another form, His glory bursting through His humanity.

Then a cloud descended—probably the Shekinah glory associated with the immediate presence of God. The cloud covered them all. The disciples were terrified as they entered into the cloud. It was then—most certainly for their benefit that they heard God's voice, "This is My Son, whom I love; with him I am well pleased. Listen to him!" (Matthew 17:5) What privilege to be given a glimpse of Christ's pre-incarnate glory radiating the light of deity (John 1:14; Phil. 2:6-7). Perhaps they had grown so familiar with Jesus' humanity, they had forgotten all about His deity. Now they had been dramatically reminded that Jesus had clearly been honored by God above—Moses representing the Law, and Elijah representing the Prophets.

Reader 2 ▪ When the cloud had gone the Bible says, "the disciples saw Jesus only." With a touch the Lord indicated it was time to return to the "real world." The valley and a demon-possessed boy and a distraught father and frustrated disciples waited for them to come down from their spiritual "high."

Of course that is what spiritual mountaintops are for: to have a heavenly experience with the Lord Jesus. Perhaps after that we, like the disciples, will see "Jesus only" instead of "Jesus and," Then and only then will we be ready for whatever is waiting for us in the valley!

Three years later, as Jesus was about to enter Jerusalem, He clearly predicted His death to a crowd of people. Jesus' midnight hour was getting near. "My heart is troubled, Father," Jesus prayed out loud, "but what should I say—save Me from this hour? No, it was for this very reason I came to this hour." And then, "Father, glorify Your name." Once again God spoke from heaven, "I have glorified it, and I will glorify it again" (John 12:23-28). As the people around Him reacted, to the divine Voice, Jesus simply said, "This voice was for your benefit, not mine."

It's amazing to me that even when God had spoken in such a supernatural way, still people disbelieved. Even a voice from heaven and a perfect human life didn't convince them of the uniqueness of Jesus!

Reader 3 ▪ Jesus was able to say unequivocally, "I seek not to please myself but him who sent me" (John 5:30). In fact, Jesus always pleased God before He pleased Himself. But He was not always able to please men! Neither did He try. First and foremost, He was a God pleaser and not a self or man pleaser.

So what was God so pleased with when He looked with such favor on His Son? Basically with His willing, obedient heart; with His holy, loving life; and with His sweet, servant spirit.

He was an obedient Son denying Himself legitimate comforts and rewards in order to do the Father's business. If Jesus had been a self pleaser, He would never have left heaven, where He was worshiped, for earth, where He was crucified! He would have chosen to live in a palace instead of a manger, used His powers to His own advantage, and lived a lot longer than 33 years! He didn't please Himself and He didn't always please men, not even those in His own family. He was never a crowd pleaser either, for He knew that crowds are fickle and not to be trusted at all. One day they can cry "Hosannah" and the next day "Crucify"!

Leader ▪ It's nice if people are pleased with a holy, obedient servant lifestyle, but for Jesus and for us we must not expect it. This *is* our Father's world, but there is still a Prince of this world that, though cast down, is not yet cast out. He will resist Christ's rule and reign every step of the way that he can.

If we would be like Jesus our Savior and Lord, we will need to start with a conscious decision to please Him. First and foremost, we need to pray for a life focus that is determined (God enabling us) to say as He said, "I do always those things that please Him." I will need to determine to be a God pleaser and not a self pleaser or man

18

pleaser. To live such a set apart, obedient servant lifestyle may well result in much self sacrifice and suffering, but why should the servant be above his master or the one taught higher than his teacher or the one saved superior to his Savior? Surely our aim should be to know we, too, are beloved by the Father, who finds great delight in us.

PRAYING IT THROUGH (20 MINUTES)

1. Praise God for Jesus' life. (5 minutes)

2. Pray for Christians to be God pleasers, not men pleasers. (5 minutes)

3. Pray for obedience to become the hallmark of the church of Jesus Christ. (5 minutes)

4. Pray for a sweet, servant spirit for God's leaders. (5 minutes)

Leader ▪ closes in prayer after explaining Tool Chest.

■   ■   ■

TOOL CHEST (A SUGGESTED OPTIONAL RESOURCE)

Give Me An Answer by Cliffe Knechtle. InterVarsiry Press, 1986.

Similar to *Know Why You Believe, Give Me An Answer* takes on the tough questions unbelievers often ask us. Its breadth is wide in that it tackles 40 questions people have thrown at Knechtle during his open-air evangelism on college campuses. Some examples follow:

Why do you say that Jesus Christ is the only way to God?
Isn't it enough to lead a good life?
Is there really going to be a hell?
How could a loving God send people to hell?
Should I accept Jesus just so I won't go to hell?
Are those who never heard about Christ going to hell?
Why do innocent people suffer?
Shouldn't God bear the responsibility for allowing evil to exist?
Why are there so many hypocrites in the church?

Isn't Christianity a crutch for weak people?
Isn't the Resurrection a myth?
What's wrong with sex if you're in love?
What's wrong with homosexuality?
Can't I wait and accept Christ later?

This is a handy tool to have on your shelf for letter writing as well as conversation, and a great gift for a high school graduate or college student.

Jesus' Temptations

. . .

Leader ▪ welcomes everyone and asks someone to open in prayer and another to read Luke 4:1-13. Designates three readers.

Leader ▪ asks:

1. Where did Jesus begin His ministry, and why is this unusual? Although Luke is writing to a Gentile, what would a Jewish audience have associated with the 40 days Jesus spent in the wilderness? (Deut. 8:2) Contrast the behavior, attitude, and result of the wilderness experience for Israel and for Jesus.

2. How does Jesus test the credibility of the devil's suggestions? (cf. Deut. 8:3; 6:13; 6:16) What do you think the Son of God learned from the wilderness temptations that the ancient Israelites failed to learn?

FOOD FOR THOUGHT

Reader 1 ▪ After His baptism Jesus was "led by the Spirit into the desert to be tempted by the devil." We are not to think Jesus was cowering behind a rock while Satan hunted Him down! Rather Jesus, led by the

Spirit, went into the desert to track down the arch
enemy of the human race. He forced him to attack
in order to overcome him.

Reader 2 . The origins of Satan are traced to the highest
heaven. It seems that Satan had been one of the
highest ranking angels. READ Ezekiel 28:14-15

At some point he allowed himself to become jeal-
ous of God. At once a terrible longing to be like
God—to take His place, even to have God worship
him—became a diabolical obsession. When he was
confronted with God in the form of Jesus of
Nazareth, his words reveal his great and evil ambi-
tion—"bow down and worship me"! (Matthew
4:9) But it is impossible for a created being to rise
to a higher point or level than that for which he
was created.

Satan is not the eternal equivalent to God. "He
belongs to an order of beings called Satan—not an
order of beings called God" (Timothy M. Warner,
Spiritual Warfare, Crossway Books, 1991, pp.
28-30). Tim Warner also points out that angels are
as it were God's "staff" to run the world—so the
angels Lucifer took with him in his fall from
heaven are like disgruntled employees out to get
the boss! God, however, limits what they can do
pending their final judgment (Rev. 20:10).

Satan's whole aim is to deprive God of His rightful
glory given to Him by human beings. One way he
does this is by tempting people to love the glory of
the world more than God's glory. *I'll give you
anything you want if you'll ask me instead of asking
God!* he says.

Reader 3 ▪ So what is written in the Word about all this? If we are tempted by the world we are told: "Don't love it" (1 John 2:15); by the flesh, "Don't feed it" (Philippians 3:19); or if by the devil himself—"Don't worship 'it'" (Matthew 4:10). (Whatever the "it" is, he's asking us to worship it instead of worshiping God.) Yet Satan is already a beaten foe. You and I can face him in Christ and know that "the one who is in [us] is greater than the one who is in the world" (1 John 4:4). Let's look in a little more detail at how Christ met His temptations and how because of Him we may meet and overcome ours.

Satan knew Jesus had fasted for 40 days and nights. He was well aware He was weak and hungry, and there was nowhere to buy bread. As his habit was, Satan seized such an opportunity, attacking when Jesus was weak and vulnerable. The evil one suggested that if Jesus really was God He should use His miraculous powers to satisfy His legitimate needs (Luke 4:3).

Leader ▪ On the surface it seems a very reasonable suggestion. Below the surface, however, it was a very different matter. The devil knew that Jesus had voluntarily laid His power down in obedience to God's way of getting the work of redemption done. To use His own power to help Himself instead of relying on God, who for His own reasons had not chosen to provide food for Him at that moment, would have been to negate the principle He had agreed to live by; namely, the principle of being a willing, trusting, dependent, obedient son. He would not abandon that principle. Even after fasting for 40 days and nights, obedience was more important than His urgent physical needs.

Reader 1 ▪ It's hard to do the will of God and stay hungry. Amy Carmichael, missionary to India, had a very natural, God-given, legitimate hunger. It was the need to be married and share her life and ministry with a companion. The opportunity came, and even though people urged her to take it, she recognized the Lord's voice saying, "I have something 'different' for you. Not 'better' not 'worse'—but 'different.'" It seemed to Amy that God was asking, "Are you willing to do My will and stay hungry?" It was a hard choice, but Amy Carmichael made it and stayed hungry. She never did marry and finished out her days among the Indian people whom she loved and served.

Amy realized, as we must realize, that man is so much more than a "fed animal," and sometimes our natural desires are to be left unfulfilled for the sake of the kingdom. Satan is always trying to lure us into some sort of position outside the will of God. Jesus rejected a passing satisfaction obtainable only at the cost of obedience.

Reader 2 ■ You and I must remain within the sphere of divine government. Man with God is equal to all pressure brought to bear against us and superior to all temptation. Today Satan is still trying to overthrow our obedience by directing all of our attention to our physical nature.

The second temptation Jesus was faced with was set by Satan in the city of Jerusalem. Even though Jesus was in the desert, Satan was able to take Him in vision or thought to the highest point in the temple complex. The devil suggested Jesus should throw Himself down, assuring Him God's ministering angels would catch Him and land Him unharmed. Satan was trying to get Jesus to demand miraculous protection as proof to Satan of God's love and care for Him. Jesus calmly replied, "It says: 'Do not put the Lord your God to the test'" (Luke 4:12). He meant don't test the character of God to see if He loves us by what He allows us to go through.

Reader 3 ▪ Jill Briscoe says, "I had a lady say to me once, 'God can't possibly love me. I asked Him to protect me on a journey and I finished up in a car crash!' We can and should most certainly ask God to protect us, but the appropriate attitude is 'trust and obey' whatever He allows. Dr. Leighton Ford caught himself praying for his son during a life and death operation, 'Lord, please, be good to us and let Sandy live.' He realized almost as soon as the prayer was prayed that God was good whether Sandy lived or died!"

Leader ▪ Even though Satan attacked Jesus' perfect confidence in God, Jesus was calmly content with going home the rugged way. And He never once lost His faith in the love and goodness of God! Satan, of course, was not adverse to using Scripture if it suited his purposes. He didn't, however, know the Scriptures as well as Jesus!
G. Campbell Morgan says, "It is a revelation of our Lord's mastery of the weapon. In comparison with Christ the devil was a poor swordsman when he attempted to use the sword of the Spirit. It would seem as though with quiet and yet mighty movement of His strong arm Jesus wrestled the sword from Satan" (*The Crises of the Christ*, p. 154).

This temptation was also an attempt to get the Lord to use His God-given powers to His own temporal advantage. J.W. Stott says Jesus was tempted to use His gift for His own aggrandizement. We can worship our own gift, or popularity, too, and hear Satan laughing all the way home to hell. We must not worship, or rely on, ourselves or any being other than God to do His work.

Reader 1 ▪ The third temptation is perhaps the one we can most easily recognize. "Worship me," says Satan, throwing all subtlety to the winds! "And I'll give you the world." Satan claimed that all the kingdoms of the world were snoozing in his arms. In a sense it is true, whether people know it or not. The world's people are mostly "under his sway." Satan is, as Jesus dubbed him, the prince of this world. BUT JESUS IS KING.

The scene was a high mountain. "In a moment" we are told, Satan caused all the glory of the world's kingdoms to flash in front of Jesus. He invited Jesus to take a shortcut. "Be King without a crown of thorns—do it my way," he said. Be King for a day! Jesus, however, knew He was to worship God only and be obedient to redeem humanity God's way. A path that ran right through Calvary! So Jesus answered with authority: "Do not put the Lord your God to the test."

Leader ▪ Some in the early church were sidetracked into worshiping angels, good forces, or "higher powers." To worship either good or bad forces instead of worshiping God is to bow down to Satan, and, of course, to worship Satan, himself is expressly forbidden. Satan offers occult powers to any person who asks and gives him the control he wants. Jesus left the control of people, His circumstances, and future in God's hands where they rightfully belong! Jesus met this test as He had all the others, in the power of the Holy Spirit and with the Word of God. So can we.

1. How might this third temptation have prepared Jesus for what He was going to have to face in Gethsemane and at Golgotha? (Matt. 16:21-23; Luke 22:39-46;)

2. According to Luke 4:1-13, what is the extent of the devil's dominion?

3. Was Jesus ever rid of the devil and temptation in His life and ministry? (cf. Luke 4:13; 10:18; 13:16; 22:31; Heb. 4:15)

Reader 2 ▪ The Word is indispensable, the Spirit is essential—prayer is imperative and the armor of faith an absolute necessity. So when the devil tries to divert attention or tempts us to be "Queen for a Day," or when we fall to temptation and sin and feel sick with ourselves for it, remember Jesus has met and dealt with the devil. When the devil had finished tempting Jesus, he left Him "for a season" and angels came and ministered to Him.

Reader 3 ▪ After a season of temptation the angels will touch and restore you as even they came to Jesus. If you have fallen, God will forgive you if you ask Him to and clean you up on the inside. That is such a great feeling. So take the sword of the Spirit and let's be up and at 'em.

Leader ▪ leads

TALKING IT OVER (30 MINUTES)

1. Which temptation can you best identify with? What do you do when you are tempted? Does the Bible help? Share the helps you have received. (10 minutes)

2. Read 1 Corinthians 10:13. Discuss.

- the promise in it.
- the comfort in it.
- the warnings in it.

(10 minutes)

3. What steps do you take if you fall into temptation? Read Psalm 51 and write down the steps David took. *(10 minutes)*

PERSONAL APPLICATION

1. Do you live by the Word of God? Does it nourish and sustain you?

2. What example does Jesus set for confronting temptation? Did He use any resource unavailable to us?

3. Is the devil an actual person to Jesus? (cf. Luke 8:12; 10:18; 11:18; 13:16; 22:31) Is he a person to you?

4. Is temptation sin?

SYNOPSIS

Write a brief synopsis of Jesus' heartbeat when facing temptation.

PRAYING IT THROUGH (5 MINUTES EACH)

1. Praise God for His victory over Satan at Calvary.

2. Read and meditate on Colossians 2:6-15.

    - silent thanksgiving for the promises in these verses.

3. Pray for God's

    - missionaries
    - Christian educators and their families who are under special attack today
    - leaders

4. Pray for people you know under attack (first names only).

5. Pray for your own families needs.

6. Finish by praising Him for His answers. Use Psalm 2 if you wish.

DIGGING DEEPER

1. How did Christ spend His time, and how might this have prepared Him for the future?

2. How does the devil address Jesus? In light of Luke 3:22, what is the devil challenging and attempting to undermine?

3. Examine all three temptations and state what is at the heart of each in your own words. What conflict would Jesus have suffered in deciding what was the right thing to do in each case? What was the devil asking Him to compromise in each?

FOR FURTHER STUDY

1. Do a synoptic study (compare the Gospel accounts) on the temptation of Jesus. What do the other Gospels include that Luke does not, and what do they omit that Luke mentions?

2. Read *Spiritual Warfare* by Timothy Warner.

CHAPTER FOUR

Jesus' Ministry

. . .

Leader ▪ opens by inviting input from last lesson. Recap and revisit things learned from the temptations of Jesus.

Leader ▪ designates three readers. Asks someone to read Luke 4:14-30

FOOD FOR THOUGHT

Leader ▪ leads:

Jesus, led by the Spirit into the Judean desert, overcame Satan's temptations to abandon the plan of redemption. After this, Jesus began traveling around His own area preaching, teaching, and healing. It was a very successful first campaign. At the conclusion of it, He came home to Nazareth and went to the synagogue on the Sabbath. He was given the honor of reading the Scriptures—He read loudly and clearly:

> "The Spirit of the Lord is on me,
> because has anointed me
> to preach good news to the poor.

He has sent me to proclaim freedom for the prisoners
and recovery of sight for the blind,
to release the oppressed,
to proclaim the year of the Lord's favor."

Reader 1 ■ Then He simply said, "Today this scripture is fulfilled in your hearing" and sat down. The understatement of the year—the Scripture says, "every eye was fixed on Him." In effect, the Carpenter was claiming to be the Christ. The man was saying, "I am the Messiah, the long-awaited Deliverer." Reading the people's minds, the Son of God reminded them "no prophet is accepted in his hometown" (Luke 4:24).

With howls of rage, the erstwhile friends and neighbors of "Joseph's son" grabbed Him, rushed Him outside the town, which was built on a cliff, and tried to throw Him over the edge. But God had not planned that Jesus' ministry would end before it even began! His time had not come. With the imposing authority that was to earmark His incredible three years of ministry, the Bible says Jesus simply "walked right through the crowd and went on His way" (Luke 4:30). In such a way Jesus' public ministry began!

Leader ■ leads discussion

1. Jesus received varied responses from the outset of His ministry. Categorize these (Luke 4:22, 28-29, 32, 36-37, 42; 5:8-11, 17-19, 21, 26).

2. In the synagogue, Jesus read from Isaiah 61:1-2a, a Messianic prophecy describing the ministry of the Messiah. What was the content of His preaching? What was Jesus claiming?

3. What two illustrations does Jesus employ, and what is He proving by them? Why were the people of Nazareth

offended, and how badly were they offended?

Reader 2 ▪ Jesus was not a globetrotter. During the following two to three years He stayed within an area approximately 125 by fifty miles and most of the time worked in a very small part of that region. He quickly became extremely popular. But He resisted every attempt to anchor His activity to an earthly agenda.

The second phase of His ministry was spent meeting human needs, preaching, and teaching. He traveled in areas that were not as politically volatile as other areas, gathering a group of men around Him—teaching and training them. His disciples had a chance to follow Him, learn from Him, and serve Him.

Leader ▪ leads

TALKING IT OVER (10 MINUTES)

1. If you had lived in Jesus' day and were a:

    ▪ Jew ...

    ▪ Gentile ...

    ▪ Roman ...

    . . . what would have convinced you Jesus was who He said He was? Discuss.

    If you had been one of the 12 disciples:

    ▪ which miracle would have convinced you, and why?

    ▪ which sermon would have convinced you, and why?

    (10 minutes)

PRAYING IT THROUGH (10 MINUTES)
On Your Own

1.   Choose one of Jesus' miracles to think about. Shut your eyes and "see" the story happen. Then thank Him for it. Talk to Him about it. Apply it in prayer to your own life. (5 minutes)

In a Group

2.   Think of one person who needs the ministry of Jesus. Someone sick, discouraged, desperate. Pray for them (first names only). (5 minutes)

Leader ■ encourages group to think of the principle of dependence.

Leader ■ asks "Do you try to take matters into our own hands too often? Spend time praying as a group that you can live by Christ—as he lived by the Father."

PRAYER TIME

Pray Jesus' teaching will get into the whole world.

Leader ■ uses:

PERSONAL APPLICATION

1.   How do people in general respond to Jesus today?

2.   Do most people understand the claims He made?

3.   Now that you know who He claimed to be, what is your response?

Reader 3 ■ The third phase of Jesus' ministry began with a growing confrontation with the religious leaders of His day. This phase ended with His terrible death at the hands of the Roman authorities. And yet, Rome did not take His life. Nor did the Pharisees.

He came to die. He laid His life down deliberately and in accordance with a divine plan. He said, "The reason my Father loves me is that I lay down my life—only to take it up again. No one takes it from me, but I lay it down of my own accord. I have authority to lay it down and authority to take it up again" (John 10:17-18).

Leader ■ asks:

What conflict begun in Luke 4:1-13 is continued in 4:33-36 and 41? What recognition did the demons have?

Reader 1 ■ The men who lived the closest to Jesus throughout His three years of tumultuous ministry were so convinced of His deity, they not only left everything dear to them to follow Him, but were willing to go to Jerusalem and die with Him for their convictions. And that after being warned about the kind of death they might well share with their Master. So let's take a look at three aspects of Jesus' ministry that gives us proof of His identity beyond all reasonable doubt.

Reader 2 ■ First of all, He was a master teacher. But Jesus' teaching cannot be followed without Jesus' power. We cannot live the Christian life without the Christ who lived it. His teaching was quite different from the rabbis'; His aim was to get His followers to grasp the basic principles and use discretion and initiative in passing on what they had learned.

The orthodox teachers were unsettled by the very idea of grasping the "spirit of the Law" rather than the letter. Bolstered by all their rules and regulations, they constantly tried to enforce them all by intimidation. But even when the synagogues were not particularly welcoming to the preacher from

Nazareth, the grassy slopes around Galilee made a natural amphitheater around the beautiful lake and became a great place to accommodate the thousands of common people who came to hear Him.

Reader 3 ▪ Jesus continued His ministry, concentrating on the disadvantaged. He had claimed, "I've come to bring good news to the poor," and so to the poor He came. The disreputable flocked around Him, too. They saw His holiness, and yet were sure of His forgiveness and acceptance. He obviously enjoyed their company. The tax collectors, the scabs of their time; prostitutes; and dropouts flocked to hear Him. He told them their sins were forgiven with such authority they didn't doubt it and heard His command to go and "sin no more" with a genuine desire to obey Him. Because of the company He kept, He was called by the hierarchy a "glutton, drunkard, and a friend of tax collectors and sinners." Even the demented and those possessed by evil spirits recognized Jesus.

That was one thing about Jesus—you could never be neutral or indifferent. Here was a man who, as even His enemies noted, the whole world had apparently hailed as Messiah. He healed blind eyes, opened deaf ears, straightened crippled legs, and even raised the dead!

Leader ▪ asks a question. "Do you believe Jesus was God? If so, tell him!"

Leader ▪ leads group in silent prayer then invites group—still in silent prayer—to pray for those they know who do not believe in the deity of Christ.

Leader ▪ reads:

36

When it was time to go to Jerusalem, Jesus had become a household name. The people knew the Pharisees and Sadducees were angry and hostile toward Him, and they themselves were divided in their opinions. Some said He was a prophet, others the Christ, still others—following the official line—an imposter (John 7:40).

In the middle of the controversy, Jesus arrived in Jerusalem. Then temple guards were dispatched to arrest Him but returned empty-handed, lamely explaining to their superiors, "No one ever spoke the way this man does" (John 7:46).

Meanwhile, taking full use of His opportunities to speak to thousands of people who had come to Jerusalem for the festival, Jesus preached one of His most famous sermons.

"I am the Light of the world—people who follow Me won't walk in darkness," He said. "Follow Me home," He invited mankind. "I'll show you the way. Yes, the world is dark, but I am light."

Now the heat was turned up. The leaders of the Jews grew really frightened as well as angry. " 'Look how the whole world has gone after Him,' they said to one another" (John 12:19). "We must get rid of Him." And so, the confrontation began in earnest.

Reader 1 ▪ Jesus explained over and over again. "The Father in Me does the work," He said. And then, to His disciples, "As I live by the Father, so you are to live by Me—for without Me you can do nothing." Here lies the principle of the Christian life. If Jesus did nothing without depending on the Father, we certainly can't do anything without depending on Him! What did Jesus depend on His Father for? First of all, He depended on Him for direction in His life. Before any big decision, He withdrew to pray and seek God's will.

Reader 2 ▪ Second, Jesus depended on His Father to affirm Him. We have already seen that Jesus lived to please the Father and not Himself or other people, but He often got discouraged just as we do. When His friends forsook Him and fled, He turned to His Father for comfort and strength. And so might we. As He lived by the Father, so we are to live by Him! There will be times when we are reviled and must bless, or are forsaken and must walk on alone. We will need to lean heavily on our unseen Guide and Friend for strength.

Reader 3 ▪ Then Jesus depended on His Father for words. It seems a strange concept, doesn't it? If Jesus was God, why did He need to depend on anyone? Here again we come face-to-face with the gigantic mystery. Jesus laid aside His independence and chose to become a willing, obedient Son, fully dependent on the Father for everything. This voluntary humility was acted out in the human person that God became!

Jesus depended on His Father for dynamic. For power! If Jesus depended on God to raise the dead and His Father heard and answered Him, we too can depend on God to bring eternal life to spiritually dead people we know. "Nothing is too hard for the Lord."

Leader ▪ Jill Briscoe says, "Thirty-five years after Christ raised my soul to new life, I'm still learning to live by Jesus as Jesus lived by God. It takes a lifetime to learn dependency, but it's worth every minute of it! His words are mine for the asking. His strength mine for the taking. His heart mine for the wanting. His love mine for the knowing. Faith and obedience are twin pillars of belief that can lift our Christianity high above mundane religiosity—and give us life more abundant!"

1. Discuss the principle of dependency in the Christian life.

   ▪ What does it mean?

   ▪ What doesn't it mean?

   ▪ Give an example from your own life.

   (10 minutes)

DIGGING DEEPER

1. Read Luke 4:14–5:39. What several elements of Jesus' ministry does Luke showcase?

2. How does Luke build upon one of the major themes of Jesus' ministry in Luke 4:14, 18? (see Luke 1:35, 41; 2:25, 27; 3:16, 22; 4:1) How does he illustrate this characteristic in chapter 4 of his Gospel account? By what authority and power did Jesus teach and heal? (Luke 4:36)

3. What further claims did Jesus make in chapter five (vv. 10, 20-24, 31, 36-39)? How were these claims received?

4. Reread Luke 4 and 5. What is Luke stressing? What does he want his readership to be certain of, to grasp?

Leader ▪ summarizes the heartbeat of Jesus' ministry and message to end the lesson. Recommends book from the tool chest.

■ ■ ■

TOOL CHEST *(A SUGGESTED OPTIONAL RESOURCE)*

Reinventing Evangelism: New Strategies for Presenting Christ in Today's World by Donald C. Posterski. InterVarsity Press, 1989.

Posterski's thesis is that the world has changed so incredibly that our old tracts, formulas, and Gospel presentations have become oblique. They are outdated, uniformed, simplistic and do not speak to the issues, needs, and appetites of our secular society. Major shifts have occurred within our culture, and consequently, our approaches to and assumptions about evangelism must be challenged, redefined, and redesigned. Christianity must be presented in a credible manner which does not insult the intelligence of our peers. What do they actually observe that we have to offer besides, as Posterski exclaims, "a privatized faith experience and some new social contacts?" The Christian foundations under our culture are crumbling. The social consensus has gone against us. And Christianity is fast losing its reputation for the ability to make a difference. Posterski provides a fascinating, disquieting exploration of these trends, with strategies based on scriptural principles for effectively sharing Christ with and making a difference in today's world.

CHAPTER FIVE

Jesus in Gethsemane

■ ■ ■

Leader ▪ welcomes study group and invites needs and struggles to be expressed in an opening time of prayer.

DISCOVERY TIME (*10 MINUTES*)

1. Read

    ▪ Matthew 26:36-43

    ▪ Mark 14:32-41

    ▪ Luke 22:39

    ▪ John 18:1

    Make a list of all the things that happened in Gethsemane (there are some things in one Gospel you will not find in another).

Leader ▪ explains the group will discover the facts deductively together.

DIGGING DEEPER

1. What is the setting for this occasion which the other gospel writers refer to as Gethsemane? What events surround this

experience? Jesus was preparing Himself spiritually, emotionally, and physically for what traumas?

2. What does the Lord imply that He is praying for Himself? (cf. Luke 22:48, Heb. 2:18, 4:15) Who is being tested, and what is the temptation?

3. How real was Jesus' struggle against temptation, and what metaphor points to its sincerity? What experience prepared Him for this moment? (Review chapter 3 of this Bible study guide.) Who is not mentioned here, but by implication must be present contesting Jesus? (cf. Luke 4:13)

4. Look ahead in chapter 23. Where does Jesus encounter His greatest agony? Where is His personal battle for our redemption fought?

5. How did Judas know where to find Jesus? What habit did Jesus have?

6. Describe the final choice the Lord makes (cf. Phil. 2:5-11).

Leader ■ chooses three readers.

FOOD FOR THOUGHT

Reader 1 ▪ Jill Briscoe recounts, "I was visiting my grandchildren. It was Thanksgiving time and I had inadvertently asked, "What do you want for Christmas?" The four smallest children—all under six years of age—flew to a drawer where Mommy kept a toy catalog and began shouting, "I want this—and this and this, please Nanna." Imagine how surprised I would have been if the kids had answered my question with, "It's not what *I* want, Nanna—what do *you* want to give us?" Well now, I guess we'd have to have 'perfect' children for that to happen, wouldn't we? And though they are 'near perfect'—I had no such response!"

When Satan asked Jesus in Gethsemane what He wanted for Easter, none of us would have blamed Jesus for answering "life." But, in fact, the perfect Son of God answered, "It's not what I want but what my Heavenly Father wants that matters. His will, not Mine be done."

Reader 2 ▪ Gethsemane was a beautiful place that Jesus loved to retreat to, to regroup, talk to His Heavenly Father, and be fortified—to do the Father's will. Many times we find ourselves in a Gethsemane. We struggle to want what He wants. But how do we want what God wants? Jill Briscoe says, "It has been my experience that half of me "wants" to do what I know I should do, but the other half of me doesn't 'want' any part of it. It's as if I am willing my will to do the right thing, but my emotions have their hands over their ears!"

Our emotions are somewhat like clamoring children, loudly demanding their own way, while our will can be likened to a good mother patiently seeing that her will is done and the right course of action is taken *despite* the cries of her little ones. As the mother gently but persistently insists on her own way, the children eventually fall into line. The will that has joined hands with the will of God must be like the good mother, patient to see to it the right thing is done but must not allow the *children* to rule her. We all know what confusion follows if children take over the adult role. Those whose wills have made a decision to will God-ward—along His will—will find their own emotions clamoring against that decision every day of their lives.

Reader 3 ▪ Jesus had lived the whole of His life conforming to the divine purpose. He was able to say, "I do always what pleases Him." Have you seen to it that your hands have joined hands with the purpose and will of God for your life? Once your will is in God's hands, you will join Him in fulfilling His purposes, whatever your feelings feel!

But, you may wail—how long will it take for my feelings to fall in line? Somehow we have no stomach to do anything that isn't fueled by feelings. It is in our own particular Garden of Gethsemane that God has provided strength for us. In prayer I can battle through issues to a divine and eternally good conclusion.

Reader 1 ▪ Jesus, having arrived in the Garden with His disciples, asked the 11 to stay put while He and James, John, and Peter went to pray. The three disciples promptly fell asleep—the Gospel says they were worn out "from sorrow" (Luke 22:45). Jesus, needing their support, woke them up and warned them about the trials ahead of them all and said, "The spirit is willing, but the body is weak" (Matthew 26:41).

He went away and prayed the same prayer as before.
Jesus was in agony. Not physical agony—that would
come later—but spiritual agony, knowing what it
would mean to bear the sin of the whole world for
us (Matthew 26:37-39). "My Father, if it is possible,"
Jesus prayed, "may this cup be taken from Me. Yet
not as I will, but as You will." Jesus knew God's will
"must be done" and it must be done by Him. There
was no one else big enough, good enough, powerful
enough to deal with sin. Only God could do that. In
Scripture the cup is usually used as a metaphor for
suffering. As His death was unique, so was His
anguish. Our best response to His tears is at least
hushed worship.

Reader 2 ▪ First of all, if we are planning to will to do His will,
we, like Him, will need to find a place to go. A
garden called Gethsemane. Saint Luke tells us He
went "as usual" to the garden. Is there a garden
where we go "as usual"?

Jill Briscoe shares, "I think of a hill behind our
house in England. It was there surveying all I loved
most about my homeland, laid out in the green,
green countryside I battled through the conflicts
arising in my heart concerning immigration. It was
hard to leave it all behind to come to the U.S.A. I
found out I was more English than I knew! That
soft, quiet hillside was my Gethsemane!"

Leader ▪ All of us need to pick a place. A quiet spot in the middle of
all the hassles of life, where we can pull ourselves alongside
the will of God for our lives. Then we must find people to
take with us—prayer partners that will not, like the disciples, fall asleep on the job. This will necessitate us making
plans, plans for a regular devotional life that we can put
into effect. If we have had one and have quit because of
lapsed devotional disciplines, we need to institute it again.

1. What model does Jesus provide for combating temptation? (1 Cor. 10:13; Heb. 4:15-16)

2. Do you have a habit of regular prayer and a pattern for meeting with Christians to pray?

3. How has God strengthened you in times of crisis?

4. Can we ever experience the depth of struggle and distress Jesus experienced at Gethsemane? Why, or why not?

5. Are you preparing yourself to face the temptations and trials you will face in the future? What would Jesus have to say to you today?

6. What did the Lord Jesus do for you in Gethsemane?

7. What posture for prayer did Jesus assume? What does His position reveal about His attitude?

8. How are the disciples pictured in this account? What concern does Jesus have for them, and how does He

instruct them to protect and strengthen themselves for what is to come? While alive, what are Jesus' final directions to the Twelve as a whole?

But what do I do with my time in Gethsemane you may ask?

God has a personal agenda for each of us, and the Bible is a great place to look to find it explained. Maybe it will not be spelled out in particulars, but it certainly will be outlined in principle. For instance, "You shall not covet your neighbor's wife" is a principle (Exodus 20:17). This imperative included not only your own wife but your friend's wife, your bosses' wife, and anyone else's wife! The principle is personal integrity concerning other people's possessions and property. God tells us we are not to take anything that belongs to our neighbor. We need to apply that prohibition in particular to our own circumstances as different situations arise.

So we will need to get acquainted with God's "Thou shalt nots." Then we need to apply His general principles to our particular situation.

Reader 3 ■ So there will be times in all of our lives when, like Jesus, we will have a "Gethsemane" experience. Perhaps with "strong crying and tears." We too may wrestle with a "cup" of suffering we know He is asking us to drink. But we can know plainly that— having asked Him if there is "any other way" we can go; and having received a negative heavenly answer, we say, "not my will but Thine be done"— God will assist us in whatever it is we need to do.

Jill Briscoe tells, "When we received the call to our present church over twenty years ago, there were many difficulties facing us as a family in regard to that decision. Both Stuart and I had widowed mothers to think about. Who would look after them, and how could we both continue to take our share of responsibility 2,000 miles away?

"There was one thing I was *dreading* doing. Telling my widowed mother. Knowing her inordinate fear of flying, I knew she would never come and visit us (which she didn't), might not understand our biblical reasoning for our decision because she had missed out on Scripture training (which we hadn't), and might be so totally devastated at suffering another great loss.

"Being in my own Gethsemane was one thing—causing someone else to experience a cup of suffering was another! It was one of the hardest things I ever did. There was grief and there were tears. There were soft words and lots of kisses and hugs. God strengthened me for those words I needed to speak, and He strengthened Mother too. He was with me as I broke the news and had prepared Mother ahead of time to receive it.

"When you have the "cup" in your hand, it helps to think about Gethsemane. Whatever cup of suffering it is that God asks us to drink, .:we can know it could "never" be a cup like His, and it will never need to be drunk "alone." It's not so hard, you know, when you see Him in your mind's eye in Gethsemane for you—it's not so hard at all."

Leader ▪ suggests Homework and explains Tool Chest.

HOMEWORK

1. What is cup symbolic of in the Scriptures? (cf. Isa. 51:22; Mark 10:38)

2. What is often associated with the cup in the Old Testament? (cf. Isa. 51:17; Jer. 25:15-17, 28-29; Lam. 4:21-22; Ezra 23:32-34; Hab. 2:16)

3. Now what temptation do you think Jesus faced? Is He afraid of death? (cf. Mark 15:34; 2 Cor. 5:8)

PRAYER TIME (30 MINUTES)

1. Choose one of the Gospel records and read it to yourself. Then—

    ▪ praise God for Jesus' victory in Gethsemane.

    ▪ pray about keeping awake to pray—both physically and spiritually.

    (10 minutes)

2. Pray for those who are trying to compromise the will of God and get their own way.

    (10 minutes)

3. Pray for—

    ▪ the prayer life of your church.

    ▪ each other's prayer life.

    ▪ your children's prayer life.

    (10 minutes)

Leader ▪ closes in prayer.

■ ■ ■

TOOL CHEST (A SUGGESTED OPTIONAL RESOURCE)

So Great Salvation: Understanding God's Redemptive Plan by J.J. Strombeck. Kregel Publications, 1992.

In simple terms, Strombeck lays out God's incredible plan and work of salvation. He explains why our salvation is so great and so important, what it is we have been delivered from, how God's justice was completely satisfied, and what our relationship is now like with God. He also defines how Christ Jesus accomplished our redemption, its certainty, eternal nature, and the consequences of neglecting this great salvation.

Mr. Strombeck had effective ministry with Dallas Theological Seminary, InterVarsiry Christian Fellowship, Moody Bible Institute, and Young Life. He had a heart for foreign missions and invested in the instruction of students in God's Word so that they might share that Word around the world.

CHAPTER SIX

Jesus' Crucifixion

•   •   •

Leader ▪ welcomes group, designates three readers, and asks someone to read scripture.

Read Isaiah 53.

▪ Work your way through the chapter.

▪ Which verses correspond to a particular incident in
Jesus' trial and crucifixion? (e.g., v. 3 "He was despised
and rejected by men. . ." corresponds to Jesus being
rejected by the Jews at His trial.)

The Old and New Testaments are a whole. "The new is in
the old concealed, the old is in the new revealed."

Now we will look at the New Testament.

1. Read Luke 23:1-49. Divide it into sections and title
each.

2. What motivated the Jewish leaders to condemn
Jesus? On what three accounts did they accuse Him?
Were these accusations true or falsified? (cf. Luke
20:25; 22:67ff)

3. After considering the evidence, what did both Pilate and Herod conclude? How was their relationship altered during the trial, and what may have contributed to this change?

4. How would you characterize Herod's interest in Jesus? What was his reaction when he came face-to-face with Jesus?

5. How many times did Pilate try to avoid sentencing Jesus to death? (cf. Luke 23:4, 14-15, 22; John 18:31, 38; 19:4, 6) What tactics did he use to evade the sentence?

6. What parties were putting pressure on Pilate? Why did he succumb? Who may have incited the crowds? (cf. John 19:6-7, 12, 15) Who does Luke indicate was responsible for Jesus' death? (cf. Luke 23:10, 12, 18, 25) How did Pilate "get even" with the chief priests?

7. Contrast Barabbas and Jesus. What do Barabbas' pardon and Jesus' death foreshadow?

8. Even in death, who does Jesus identify with, and how? Who does Christ pray for with His final breaths?

9. Contrast the attitudes of the two criminals. On what basis was entrance to paradise made available or denied these men?

10. What evidence does Luke give for the voluntary nature of Jesus' death? (Luke 9:51; 23:46)

Now let's think about the absolute necessity of the cross of Christ for our salvation.

FOOD FOR THOUGHT

Reader 1 ▪ In the days Jesus lived on earth there were many forms of crucifixion—all hideous. This gruesome death was primarily designed to strip a person of every vestige of human dignity. This method of dispatching victims into eternity was introduced to the Mediterranean world from the East. Assyrian bas reliefs show how they impaled their enemies against the city walls, while in Daniel's day Darius I of Persia put down a revolt by his own people by crucifying 3,000 of his own subjects. Those were dark and cruel days and human flesh was cheap.

Israel had their own way of execution. They would throw the condemned man backward off a cliff or high place to stun him and then drop huge stones on his head. It was a somewhat more merciful way of accomplishing the death sentence. "This hanging men up alive was never before done in Israel," a Jewish writer commented.

It was left to the Romans to use crucifixion as a routine means of execution for all their conquered peoples. The idea in the minds of the Roman overlords was supposedly to deter would-be uprisings. No doubt the gruesome sight of writhing, screaming rebels set up on their crosses along side the main roads by and large had the desired effect.

Reader 2 ▪ The means of death was prolonged and excruciating. The victims were stripped naked to the jeers of the crowd that always gathered to witness a "good show." They endured a living death for hours or days depending on how badly they had been tortured beforehand. They were fastened by ropes or nails. John tells us they used nails on Jesus: They would hammer the metal spikes through the wrists, and then they would break the victims' legs and place the heels together one on the other, using one nail to fasten both. Jesus' legs, however, were not broken—perhaps to elongate His suffering or maybe to vindicate His claims—Scripture said "not a bone of Him would be broken."

Jesus died very quickly—aware to the end. When He did die it appeared to be by a deliberate act of will. Most victims cursed or screamed—Jesus died with a prayer (Luke 23:46). "No man takes my life from me, I lay it down." He had come to finish the work His Father had given Him to do (John 5:38; 17). With a shout of triumph, He told us it was finished indeed!

Max Lucado, in his excellent book *No Wonder They Call Him Savior,* says that the cross rests on the timeline of history like a compelling diamond. "My, what a piece of wood," he comments. "History has idolized it and despised it, gold plated it, burned it, worn and trashed it. History had done everything but ignore it and that is one option the cross does not offer."

Reader 3 ■ We cannot be a Christian without the Cross. That—as someone has said—is like buying a car without the engine. John Stott in *The Cross of Christ* says that "His death was central to His mission." Paul called it the core of the Gospel.

The cross tells me sin has been crossed out— dealt with. The cross tells me what a holy God thinks about my sinful nature. It must be judged. Someone has to be punished for my sin. It's either going to be me or a substitute. The cross shows us our Substitute. Jesus Christ died in our place.

You can attend church regularly, teach in the Sunday school, sing in the choir, be generous to Christian causes, but if you refuse to thank Jesus for His work of salvation you can end up shut out of heaven. You and I cannot get to heaven save through the door shaped like a cross. There is no other way. "I am the way," this Jesus claimed. The cross is therefore either the hinge or the hoax of history!!

Most of the world doesn't know what it is doing to Jesus Christ. To count Him of no worth, to misunderstand His work on the cross, to live one's life as if He never lived or died, to reject His claims to be Master over our lives, to relegate Him to a brief hour on Christmas Eve and Easter is to crucify Him as surely as the soldiers crucified Him on that hill far away. To reject Jesus is to throw away our only chance for forgiveness. If this is true then I think it would certainly be fair to say the human race certainly does not know what it is doing!

Leader ▪ One of the main problems in the area of our relationships is that of forgiveness. We sense the need in our own hearts for "someone" "somewhere" to forgive us. For "what" some of us are not sure. All we know is a gnawing sense of guilt that will not go away. We need to come to a realization this dilemma has to do with a crucified man.

Jill Briscoe says, "Fortunately, on an old wooden cross 2,000 years ago Jesus prayed for me that I would be forgiven. His prayers were answered and the cross became the pivotal turning point of my personal history as well as the history of the whole wide world—'My, what a piece of Wood!'"

Leader ▪ leads discussion and prayer time.

DISCUSSION
Can you be a Christian without the Cross?

   ▪ Yes?

   ▪ No?

   ▪ Discuss.

■ Read John 3:16. How does this verse answer the above question?

PRAYING IT THROUGH (5 *MINUTES EACH*)

1. Praise God for dying for you personally. Borrow this prayer if you don't know what to say: "Dear Lord Jesus, I believe I am the sinner You died to save. Thank You for giving Your life for me so that my sins can be forgiven. Please come into my life now by Your Holy Spirit. Thank You for hearing and answering this prayer. Amen."

    Name: _____

2. Pray for people you know who think they can get to heaven by good works, thereby bypassing the cross.

3. Pray for people undergoing persecution and trial for Christ's sake because they have tried to follow in His steps.

4. Pray that you would be able to explain John 3:16 to someone close to you who isn't a believer yet.

5. Pray that the Cross would become the motivating force of your life.

Leader ■ gives "homework" and recommends further reading from the Tool Chest.

HOMEWORK

FOR FURTHER STUDY

1. Do a word study on "paradise."

2. How did Jesus' death conform to the Father's will? (cf. John 3:16; 10:17; Mark 14:36)

3. What did Jesus' death fulfill? (cf. Mark 9:12; Luke 22:37; 24:25-27; John 13:18; 17:12; 19:23-24, 28, 36-37)

■ ■ ■

TOOL CHEST *(A SUGGESTED OPTIONAL RESOURCE)*

The Cross of Christ by John Stott, InterVarsity Press.

Now, from one of the foremost preachers and Christian leaders of our day, comes theology at its readable best, a contemporary restatement of the meaning of the cross.

At the cross, Stott finds the majesty and love God disclosed, the sin and bondage of the world exposed. More than a study of the atonement, this book brings scripture into living dialogue with Christian theology and the 20th century.

CHAPTER SEVEN

Jesus' Resurrection

. . .

Leader ▪ welcomes group and asks if anyone has a story to share about the way the Resurrection of Christ has been an encouragement. Then designates three readers and opens in prayer.

Leader ▪ leads in discovery time

DISCOVERY TIME

1. Read Luke 23:50–24:53. What does Luke emphasize in his resurrection account?

2. What information is given about Joseph's identity? What council was he a member of? (cf. Matt. 27:57; John 19:38)

3. How was Jesus' body prepared for burial? Was this adequate? What was Preparation Day? What do Luke 23:53-56 and John 19:40, 42 imply?

4. Where are the disciples during the burial? Who, in comparison, was present?

5. Who does Luke understand the two men at the tomb to be? (cf. Matt. 28:2-3, 5-7; John 20:10-13; Acts 1:10)

6. What is the point behind the angels' question, "Why do you seek the living among the dead?" What do they want the women to recall? (cf. Luke 9:22; 17:25; 18:25ff) What gave the women cause to believe?

7. How did the eleven receive the women's story? How would you describe the disciples here? Compare Peter's response. Did he believe?

8. To whom would you expect the Lord's first resurrection appearances to be directed? How does Jesus surprise you?

FOOD FOR THOUGHT

Reader 1 ▪ Good Friday is past! Things look different from the other side of the Cross. With the benefit of 2,000 years of hindsight, we understand there could be no Easter morning without a Good Friday. However, as far as the disciples of Jesus were concerned, the cross was the end of all their highest hopes and most daring dreams. The day after Calvary they were thoroughly convinced the tomb was fully occupied. The three years of service and sacrifice they had spent with Jesus seemed to have been a terrible mistake, costing themselves and their families, everything perhaps, even their very lives.

The spotlight now turns upon a councilor—a member of the ruling body—the Sanhedrin. "Joseph [was] a good and upright man, who had not consented to their [the leaders who condemned Jesus to death] decision and action" (Luke 23:50). Both Matthew and John tell us he was himself one of Jesus' disciples "but secretly because he feared the Jews" (Matthew 27:57; John 19:38). He went to Pilate and asked for Jesus' body that he might bury Him with honor. Pilate, surprised that the Lord had died so quickly, ascertained the certainty of death from the centurion in charge of the execution and, being satisfied with his report, released the body of the Lord into Joseph's hands.

Reader 2 ■ Together with Nicodemus, the two men carefully wrapped Jesus' body in linen, placing seventy-five pounds of spices between the folds of the cloth, and left the corpse in Joseph's own tomb (John 19:39; Matt. 27:59). Rolling a massive stone across the door of the sepulcher they went away aware that they must rest on the Sabbath according to their strict Jewish laws.

The leaders went to Pilate and asked that a guard be on the sepulcher. They were the first to remember that Jesus had said He would rise from the dead! "Go and make the tomb as sure as you know how," Pilate told them. And so they did.

So the only people thinking about any possible resurrection turned out to be the men who actually were responsible for His crucifixion. They might have been more than a shade uneasy remembering that not too long ago this Nazarene brought a dead man named Lazarus back to life, a man who had been dead for three whole days!

Reader 3 ■ The disciples meanwhile were too exhausted with both grief and fear to think of anything other than their immediate dilemma. Would the authorities round up the followers of Jesus, and would their fate be the same? So the women prepared for the funeral and the men who loved Jesus talked behind locked doors in hushed tones, wondering if it was safe to go back to Galilee and try to pick up what was left of their lives.

Jesus had certainly done His best to prepare His

followers for the Cross, but on at least three important occasions He had told them that after His
death on the third day He would surely rise again.
The first of those predictions was made after Peter's
great confession, "You are the Christ, the Son of
the living God." This first prediction was met with
Peter's protest and Jesus' rebuke.

The second important occasion when He addressed
the matter was as they were coming down the
Mount of Transfiguration. This time the information was greeted with a confused discussion
between Peter, James, and John. The third time
Jesus clearly told His disciples He would be raised
from the dead was as they all went up to Jerusalem
for the last time. On this occasion the Master's clear
statement that He would be crucified, buried, and
rise again the third day was met with total silence.
It seems strange that not one of the disciples
remembered these momentous promises.

Leader ▪ Part of the problem was that they really believed that Jesus
was truly dead. Perhaps they believed that the women,
crazed with grief, had carried away their Beloved. Yet,
according to the record, the women who came to the tomb
before dawn early on Easter morning came with spices in
their hands in order to bury Him and not to bear Him
away and hide Him. No, the women didn't have the body,
and the leaders didn't have it either. If they had, the
rumors of His resurrection would have burst onto the
streets of Jerusalem, and it would have all been over.

There was no question the Jewish hierarchy were
convinced the body was gone. Enough hush money was
procured for the guards who reported what happened to
the hierarchy to keep them telling lies, but they knew the
body was gone, as did the soldiers who were bribed. The
body of Jesus had been "mummified" by Joseph of

Arimathea and Nicodemus and had well and truly disappeared into thin air while sealed in a tomb and guarded by soldiers. It must be noted here the angel did not roll the stone away in order to let Jesus "out" but rather to let the women and disciples in. And yet, the empty tomb is not in itself the final audience of the resurrection of Jesus Christ from the dead.

Reader 1 ■ Peter raced to the tomb and looked inside expecting to see the corpse. What Peter saw set him "wondering" as he gazed at the grave clothes, and Scripture says seeing them he believed! What was it that convinced Peter that the body was truly gone? It was the fact that the grave clothes were left—in the shape of a body like a man-sized chrysalis after the butterfly had flown! The body, in other words, had as it were "evaporated." No wonder the Scriptures simply say "he [Peter] saw and believed"!

Thereupon sightings of the risen man who had been crucified and buried began to be rumored among his followers. The Bible says that Jesus showed Himself to people for the space of 40 days, and Paul also testified to his own dramatic encounter and conversion on the road to Damascus.

Leader ■ leads group in question time

QUESTION TIME

1. What were the two disciples discussing when the Lord Jesus appeared to them? Why didn't they recognize Him? Why do you think the Lord kept them from this knowledge at first? Was this common in His resurrection appearances? (cf. Matt. 28:17; John 20:14; 21:4)

2. How had Jesus' crucifixion affected these two disciples personally? How had it affected the community?

3. What impressed them about Jesus, and who did they blame for His crucifixion?

4. Look up the word "redeem" in a dictionary and a Bible dictionary. What did the disciples mean when they said they hoped Jesus would redeem Israel?

5. What is the content of Jesus' rebuke? What had the disciples failed to realize and accept? Notice the word "all" in Luke 24:25.

6. How did Jesus help them understand? What portions of Scripture did He use? When Jesus broke bread with them, what might have helped them recognize Him? What was their reaction?

Reader 1 ▪ Why is it so important to believe in the Resurrection? "If Christ is not risen, then is our faith vain," and if Christ is not risen, our loved ones who have already died are lost. If Jesus Christ is not raised from the dead, "we are of all men most pitiable." If Christ is risen from the dead, "He is the first fruits of those who believe." The picture Paul gives us is of the first fruits of a harvest, the promise of what is to come. He is the first fruits of God's harvest of souls—and we are the rest of the harvest.

Leader ■ leads

TALKING IT OVER (*10 MINUTES EACH*)

1. Discuss

    - Why is the Resurrection meaningful to you?

    - Why is our faith vain if Christ is not risen?

    - Read 1 Corinthians 15:55. Share what difference belief in the Resurrection has made when you have faced the death of a loved one.

2. Read 1 Corinthians 15.

    - Make a list of all the ways a resurrection body is described.

    - Which aspect encourages you, and why?

Reader 2 ■ Paul says the hope of the Resurrection is the reason he is willing to go through intense suffering for Christ. What would be the point, he asks, if Christ were not truly alive? By far the biggest problem in life is death. We spend billions of dollars trying to put off the evil day that none of us can escape. But for the Christian the stone has been rolled away from the tomb of death. It's empty! Death for the Christian is the gateway into life. Christ has gone before to tell us there is a new world ahead of us, and we can face the grave with utmost confidence in that promise.

Leader ■ leads discussion and prayer time

DISCUSSION

"Christ's death makes us fit for heaven—Christ's life makes us fit for earth." Then praise Him. (*5 minutes*)

PRAYING IT THROUGH (25 MINUTES)

1. Spend some minutes in prayer—praising God for the Resurrection. Think particularly about the characteristics of God it reveals. Praise Him for those. (10 minutes)

2. Pray for Christians who understand the cross but have failed to understand the meaning of the Resurrection for their own lives. (10 minutes)

3. Pray for preachers of the Gospel to display the joy of the Lord and His life in their ministry. (5 minutes)

   Memorize Luke 24:46-49.

Leader ■ recommends books and closes in prayer.

■ ■ ■

TOOL CHEST (A SUGGESTED OPTIONAL RESOURCE)

The Authentic Jesus: The Certainty of Christ in a Skeptical World by John R.W. Stott. InterVarsity Press, 1985.

Stott marvelously and succinctly presents contemporary criticisms of biblical Christianity and confronts these and current secular thinking regarding the person of Christ. The inadequacies of skeptics' attacks and how they contradict the Christ upheld in the Scriptures are revealed by Stott. The denial of the Virgin Birth, the bodily resurrection of Christ, and the physical nature of Christ's miracles are contested, and these accusations are answered with integrity and assuredness. Scott takes up the question, "Who is the authentic Jesus?" and proves the reasonableness of the Jesus in Scripture and of the Christian faith. It is a powerful and thought-provoking little book for the unbeliever who genuinely wrestles with such haunting doubts.

CHAPTER EIGHT

Jesus' Promise

. . .

Leader ▪ welcomes group and proposes future study plans. (See back page for other study books in this series.)

Designates three readers.

PRIMING THE PUMP

What were some of the things that Jesus had promised about the Holy Spirit, and which means the most to you?

- John 14:16-17, 20
- John 16:13

FOOD FOR THOUGHT

Leader ▪ Fast on the heels of Jesus' Resurrection came the gathering of the disciples in Jerusalem. Jesus told them to return and stay in the city until He sent them what His Father had promised—namely, the Holy Spirit, who would dress them with the dynamic they would need to preach repentance and forgiveness of sins to all nations, beginning at Jerusalem. When the great day came to experience what the

Father had promised, 120 of Jesus' disciples were all together in one place (Acts 2:1). Some of the believers had been constantly meeting together in prayer, anticipating the great day of endurment.

And then the day came! Suddenly the Holy Spirit fell on those waiting people accompanied by special supernatural phenomena. A sound "like" the blowing of a violent wind, and what "seemed to be tongues of fire" separated and came to rest on each of them (vv. 4-5). All of them were filled with the Holy Spirit and began to speak in other tongues as the Spirit enabled them! This happened so that visitors representing all the nations could hear and under- stand "the wonderful works of God." They heard these things spoken about in their own languages from men and women who had never learned to speak them and proba- bly had never heard them before themselves until that day. I wonder who was most surprised—the ones speaking the foreign languages or those hearing them.

Some had doubts about the disciples sobriety—seeking to find a reasonable answer to this extraordinary event. Peter used the opportunity, got up, and addressed the crowd pointing out that no one was drunk, since it was only 9 o'clock in the morning.

Reader 1 ▪ Peter's first sermon is a classic! Could this be the same Peter that a few weeks before couldn't keep a promise, denied His Lord with oaths and curses, and left Him to His fate? If ever there was evidence of a changed life, it was to be seen in the total transformation of Simon Peter! Jesus had promised Peter that He would make him a fisher of men (Luke 5). On the day of Pentecost, Peter "caught" 3,000 human fish. Jesus kept His promises even if Peter didn't.

During Peter's bold sermon he talked about the strange phenomena of tongues that everyone had witnessed. This is what Joel promised, he explained. Then he quoted the prophet:

> "In the last days, God says,
> I will pour out My Spirit on all people.
> Your sons and daughters will prophesy,
> your young men will see visions,
> your old men will dream dreams.
> Even on my servants, both men and women,
> I will pour out My Spirit in those days,
> and they will prophesy"
> (Acts 2:17-18).

God had poured out His Spirit as He promised He would hundreds of years previously.

Reader 2 ▪ However, someone far more important than Joel had promised that this would occur. Jesus had said so! Peter told the crowd that day that "this Jesus whom you wicked men put to death," told us while He was alive, "I am going to send you what my Father has promised." Peter must have started remembering all the times the Lord had made reference to the coming of the Holy Spirit while He was with them. He must have wondered how he could ever have missed the importance of it all.

Leader ▪ The Holy Spirit is a gracious gift of grace. A good gift given to sinful people who are sick of being sinful and are willing to repent, ask forgiveness, and receive the One who alone can make the difference and change them into God's image.

The Holy Spirit is not only a gracious gift of God but a "generating gift." He generates the power to be witnesses first in Jerusalem, then Samaria, then Judea, and then to the uttermost ends of the earth (Acts 1:8). The disciples began to witness in Jerusalem. And that's exactly where we should start as well.

Jerusalem represents the little bit of geography that lies between our own two feet at any given time. In particular it means hostile ground! It was hard for the disciples to start there: It's easy to think about going to the uttermost part of the earth; distance lends enchantment to the view. It looked frightening to contemplate taking on the Jerusalem crowd! For Jesus' friends, Jerusalem after all was a crowd that had just crucified their leader, for them the place of failure. It has been only a short time since Peter had denied his Lord in this place.

Reader 3 ▪ Now think about it. Where would the very worst place be for you to start to witness? Where do people know the worst about you? Who has heard you curse and swear and deny Christ perhaps? That's your Jerusalem—and Jesus says cheerfully it's a great place to begin to learn to be a witness.

Once we've cut our teeth in Jerusalem, we will be ready to go on to Judea. Judea was home territory for many of the disciples. In contrast to Jerusalem, Judea had been a place of success in the ministry of Jesus. A lot of people believed on Jesus in Judea. But Jesus was not visibly present anymore. Could His followers do what Jesus had done—speak as Jesus had spoken, convince people to trust God as Jesus had convinced people to trust God? Jesus had said, "Greater things than these will you do because I go to my Father." Now was the time to prove it! But what about Samaria? The Samaritans surely needed to hear some good news too. If Jerusalem was hostile ground and Judea home ground, what was Samaria? Heretical ground.

Reader 1 ▪ Jesus had a soft heart for the downtrodden and despised and for those off base theologically as the Samaritans were. The Samaritans were certainly

70

despised for that, particularly by the pious Jews. When we've fulfilled all our responsibilities in Jerusalem, Judea, and Samaria we may be called upon to go to the uttermost parts of the world. Our world we are told is a third non-Christian, a third Christianized, and a third Christian—yet even the last is made up of mostly nominal people despite almost 2,000 years passing since Jesus told His disciples to tell the world about the redemption He had accomplished. There are vast areas of our world that haven't yet heard the Gospel once.

Reader 2 ▪ Where does He want us to start? Only you can answer that question before God. But whether it be in Jerusalem, Judea, Samaria, or unto the uttermost parts of the world He has promised to endue us with power by His Holy Spirit—even as He did the disciples at Pentecost. We need to stand near enough to our Lamb to know our own heart response to the Cross, and we need to be close enough to hear the Lion of Judah's roar. Then in Max Lucado's words:

Reader 3 ▪ Something happens to a man when he stands within inches of the Judean Lion. Something happens when he hears the roar, when he touches the golden mane. Something happens when he gets so close he can feel the Lion's breath. Maybe we could all use a return visit. Maybe we all need to witness his majesty and sigh at his victory. Maybe we need to hear our own commission again. "Will you tell them?" Jesus challenged. "Will you tell them that I came back . . . and that I am coming back again?" "We will," they nodded. And they did. Will you?

Leader ■ Discuss the hardest place for you to witness, and why.

> ■ Jerusalem
>
> ■ Judea
>
> ■ Samaria
>
> ■ the uttermost parts of the world

Leader ■ leads

PRAYING IT THROUGH (*13 MINUTES*)

1. PRAISE (*5 minutes*)

    - Praise for the gift of the Holy Spirit.

    - List all the things He does for us (verbally or in writing).

    - Praise Him for all those things.

2. PRAYER (*5 minutes*)

    - Pray that the Holy Spirit will strengthen His body the church.

    - Pray that the Holy Spirit will convict and convert individuals you know.

    - Pray He will give you power to witness.

3. MEDITATE (*3 minutes*)

    - Read Matthew 28:18-20 and quietly ask God to illuminate your mind and heart about this.

Leader ■ makes the personal application.

> Have you taken the steps Peter gave his audience to become a believer? If not, take time now to confess your sins to Jesus; repent, and ask His forgiveness. Acknowledge Him as Lord and Christ, and ask for the Holy Spirit to take up residence in your heart.

Leader ■ closes in prayer.

■ ■ ■

TOOL CHEST *(A SUGGESTED OPTIONAL RESOURCE)*

My Heart—Christ's Home by Robert Boyd Munger. InterVarsity Press, 1986.

This pocket-sized booklet is a wonderful gift or stocking stuffer for both the seeker and the person who has just come to faith in Christ and must come to understand what it means to call Christ—Lord. It employs the allegory of a home to identify the many areas of our lives which must be submitted to the scrutiny and Lordship of Christ Jesus. The study, dining room, living room, workroom, rec room, bedroom, and hall closet are all described and examined for suitability and acceptability for Christ's residence in our lives. Issues of daily quiet time (i.e., Bible study and prayer), wholesome recreation, service, and standards of morality are explained and discussed. *My Heart— Christ's Home* "packs a punch" in an interesting, gentle, persuasive, and objective manner.

A Personal Note From the Author

More than to just entertain, Cook Communications Ministries hopes to inspire you to fulfill the great commandment: to love God with all your heart, soul, mind, and strength; and your neighbor as yourself. Towards that end, the author wishes to share these personal thoughts.

Heart

Ever since I became a Christian, I have made it a habit to put my questions to the biblical text, always expecting an answer to my personal and ministry dilemmas. I have never been disappointed. After partnering in mission and church with my husband for 45 years, sharing ministry with our three grown children, and having the privilege of spiritual input into the lives of 13 grandchildren, I am more convinced than ever that the Word of God applies life, truth, and reality to every heart at every age and in every situation. This knowledge has led to a passion to provide scriptural material in a format that will lead others to similar rich discoveries.

Soul

But the angel said to them, "Do not be afraid. I bring you good news of great joy that will be for all the people. Today in the town of David a Savior has been born to you; he is Christ the Lord." Luke 2:10-11

Mind

Stretch your mind by letting the scriptures speak to you. Throughout this book I have integrated the Tool Chest feature, which recom-

Strength mends excellent additional resources to develop in you the mind of Christ. Another source is John Stott's "The Cross of Christ" (InterVarsity Press), which gives us a glimpse into the heartbeat of Jesus.

As you apply these studies and put them into practice, you will discover (as I have) truth talking to your conscience during the day, peace singing you to sleep at night, and nourishment for the soul translated into action.

Oh Lord, I pray that the reader of this book will, as best as she knows how, intentionally put herself into your presence. Humble any pridefulness in her heart, and enable her to see herself as you see her. Help her to discern, find, and follow your will for her life, however difficult. Help her to change what she is, accept what she must, and endure the permitted troubles that will cause her to grow into a strong soldier of Jesus Christ.

In His Name ~ Amen